Vol. 2116

Pyotr Il'yich Tchaikovsky

Piano Collection

Album for the Young
The Seasons
The Nutcracker Suite
8 Other Selected Piano Pieces

ISBN 978-1-4950-0454-4

G. SCHIRMER, *Inc.*

Distributed By
HAL•LEONARD® CORPORATION
7777 W. Bluemound Rd. P.O. Box 13819 Milwaukee, WI 53213

Copyright © 2015 by G. Schirmer, Inc. (ASCAP) New York, NY
International Copyright Secured. All Rights Reserved.
Warning: Unauthorized reproduction of this publication is prohibited by Federal law and subject to criminal prosecution.

www.musicsalesclassical.com
www.halleonard.com

Contents

Album for the Young, Op. 39

6 Morning Prayer
7 A Winter Morning
9 The Hobby Horse
11 Mamma
12 March of the Tin Soldiers
13 The Sick Doll
14 The Doll's Burial
15 Waltz
17 The New Doll
18 Mazurka
19 Russian Song
20 The Peasant Plays the Accordion
21 Folk Song
22 Polka
23 Italian Song
24 Old French Song
25 German Song
26 Neapolitan Dance Song
28 The Nurse's Tale
29 The Witch
31 Sweet Dreams
33 Song of the Lark
35 The Organ Grinder
36 In Church

The Nutcracker Suite, Op. 71a

38 Miniature Overture
46 March
52 Dance of the Sugar Plum Fairy
56 Russian Dance, "Trepak"
59 Arabian Dance
62 Chinese Dance
64 Dance of the Reed Flutes
68 Waltz of the Flowers

The Seasons, Op. 37b

82 January: By the Hearth
88 February: Carnival
94 March: Song of the Lark
96 April: Snowdrop
100 May: Starlit Night
104 June: Barcarolle
109 July: Song of the Reaper
112 August: Harvest Song
119 September: Hunter's Song
123 October: Autumn Song
126 November: Troika
131 December: Christmas

Other Selected Piano Pieces

164 Chanson triste, Op. 40, No. 2
144 Chant sans paroles, Op. 2, No. 3
166 Chant sans paroles, Op. 40, No. 6
162 Feuillet d'album, Op. 19, No. 3
158 Humoresque, Op. 10, No. 2
154 Nocturne, Op. 10, No. 1
139 Rêverie du soir, Op. 19, No. 1
148 Romance, Op. 5

Pyotr Il'Yich Tchaikovsky
(1840–1893)

Pyotr Il'yich Tchaikovsky is regarded as the most important Russian composer of the nineteenth century. Tchaikovsky combined Russian folksong, timbres, and modes with Western form and harmonization, creating works that epitomize Russian romanticism. Many of them count among the most recognizable pieces in classical music, including *The Nutcracker*, the love theme from *Romeo and Juliet*, the opening to his Piano Concerto No. 1, and the *1812 Overture*.

Tchaikovsky was born in the small town of Votkinsk. His family moved multiple times during the first ten years of his life, first to Moscow, then to St. Petersburg, and finally to Alapayevsk, a town smaller and more remote than Votkinsk. He was able to read in French and German by the age of six, and he wrote poetry in French in addition to taking voice and piano lessons. At twelve, Tchaikovsky moved to St. Petersburg to attend the School of Jurisprudence, from which he graduated in 1859.

He took a job at the Ministry of Justice where he excelled, receiving three promotions in eight months. In the evenings, Tchaikovsky often attended the French theatre and ballet, as well as the Italian opera. He was also able to travel around the European continent on business, broadening his international perspective beyond book learning. This period in Tchaikovsky's life coincided with the rise of bourgeois music institutions, including the founding of The Russian Musical Society in 1859, which organized concerts and provided music classes to the general public. Tchaikovsky began taking music theory lessons given by the society in 1861, and in 1862 he began formal music studies at the St. Petersburg Conservatory in its inaugural semester. Tchaikovsky flourished at the conservatory, maturing rapidly as a composer under Anton Rubinstein while also studying theory, piano, flute, and organ.

Tchaikovsky graduated in 1865 and moved to Moscow to teach theory at the Moscow Conservatory. He had been recommended for the job by Nikolay Rubinstein, Anton's brother. Rubinstein was a co-founder of both the Moscow Conservatory and the Moscow branch of the Russian Musical Society. He made sure that the society's orchestra was at Tchaikovsky's disposal and he also premiered many of Tchaikovsky's piano works, ensuring that Moscow's audiences would have ample opportunity to hear the young composer's music.

In 1877, Tchaikovsky left the conservatory and gained financial independence through the help of a wealthy widow, Nadezhda von Meck. He would eventually serve as director of the Moscow chapter of the Russian Musical Society, and in 1888 he was awarded a lifetime pension from the Emperor Alexander III. Tchaikovsky died in October 1893, one week after conducting the premiere of his Sixth Symphony, of unknown causes.

Tchaikovsky's oeuvre covers all the major genres, including symphonies, program music, string quartets, piano works, instrumental concertos, songs, operas, and ballets. He admired French music, but was perhaps more influenced by Beethoven, Schubert, and Schumann, in addition to the use of timbres in orchestral writing by his Russian predecessors such as Glinka. He differed from his well-established Russian contemporaries who made up the composer consortium known as The Five. This group, which included Balakirev, Borodin, Cui, Mussorgsky, and Rimsky-Korsakov, had a nationalistic bent that caused them to shy away from the more Western models that Tchaikovsky embraced. Tchaikovsky set himself apart through a combination of idiosyncratic aspects of Russian music, sublimely emotional melodic writing, and Western European genres and forms. This allowed his music to appeal to a broader international audience, and it continues to bring joy to audiences and musicians around the world.

Album for the Young
Opus 39

ALBUM FOR THE YOUNG

1. Morning Prayer

Pyotr Il'yich Tchaikovsky
Op. 39

2. A Winter Morning

p
dim.
smorz.
p
cresc.
mf
p
cresc.
mf
dim.
p
cresc.
mf
dim.
p

3. The Hobby Horse

p
mf
p
pp

4. Mamma

Andante espressivo
p
legatissimo
cresc.
mf
p
p
mf
poco ritard.
p
p
pp

5. March of the Tin Soldiers

6. The Sick Doll

7. The Doll's Burial

8. Waltz

dimin.
p
mf
leggiero
f

9. The New Doll

10. Mazurka

11. Russian Song

12. The Peasant Plays the Accordion

13. Folk Song

14. Polka

15. Italian Song

16. Old French Song

Moderato assai

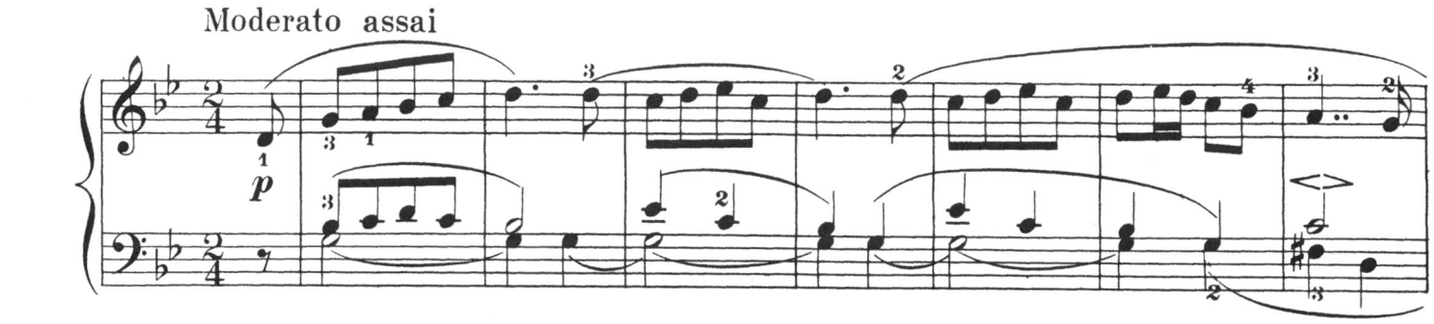

17. German Song

18. Neapolitan Dance Song

Più mosso
f
f

19. The Nurse's Tale

20. The Witch

p
f
sf
dimin.
p
mf
p
pp

21. Sweet Dreams

f
mf
f
dimin. e rit.
a tempo
p
Ped. come sopre
poco più f
p
poco rit.
a tempo
p
f
p

22. Song of the Lark

p
p
pp

23. The Organ Grinder

24. In Church

The Nutcracker Suite
Opus 71a

THE NUTCRACKER SUITE

Miniature Overture

Arranged by Stepán Esipoff
Edited by Carl Deis

Pyotr Il'yich Tchaikovsky
Op. 71a

Copyright © 1922, Renewed 1949 by G. Schirmer, Inc. (ASCAP) New York, NY
International Copyright Secured. All Rights Reserved.
Warning: Unauthorized reproduction of this publication is prohibited by Federal law and subject to criminal prosecution.

p
Ped.
mf
p
cresc.
mf
f
cresc.
f
sfz
sfz

dolce cantabile
mp
mf
sopra
p con grazia
p
cresc.
f
mp
mf
p dolce espress.
mp
p
mp
mf
f

pp
8
cresc.
ff
pesante
brillante
f
8
8

pp
pp
pp
p
p
p

p
Ped.
mf
p
p
cresc.
mf
mf
cresc.
sfz
sfz
sfz
sfz
sfz
sfz
sfz

dolce cantabile
p
sopra
p con grazia
p
cresc.
f
mf
8
p
mf
p
p
mp
f

pp
cresc.
ff
pesante
sempre ff
brillante
sfz
sfz
Ped. * Ped. * Ped. *

March

Tempo di Marcia vivo
p
mf
p
mf
p
cresc.
p subito
mf
mf
p
cresc.
mf
f
sfz

mf
mf
staccato
f
mf
staccato
mf
f
p subito
mf
p
mf
cresc.

p
mf
p
mf
p
cresc.
stacc. e leggero
f
sfz
mf
mp
f

mf
mp
f
p subito
mf
p
mf
p
cresc.
f

p subito
p
mf
p
cresc.
mf
f
sfz
mf
mf
staccato
f
mf.
staccato
mf
f

p subito
p
mf
p
mf
p
cresc.
p
mf
mf
p
cresc.
f
sfz
sfz

Dance of the Sugar Plum Fairy

mf
pp
p
sopra
sopra
sfz
pp
p
sopra
sopra
sopra
sfz
sfz
p
sfz
p
sfz
cresc.
p
ten.
ten.
f
quasi arpa
Ped.
*

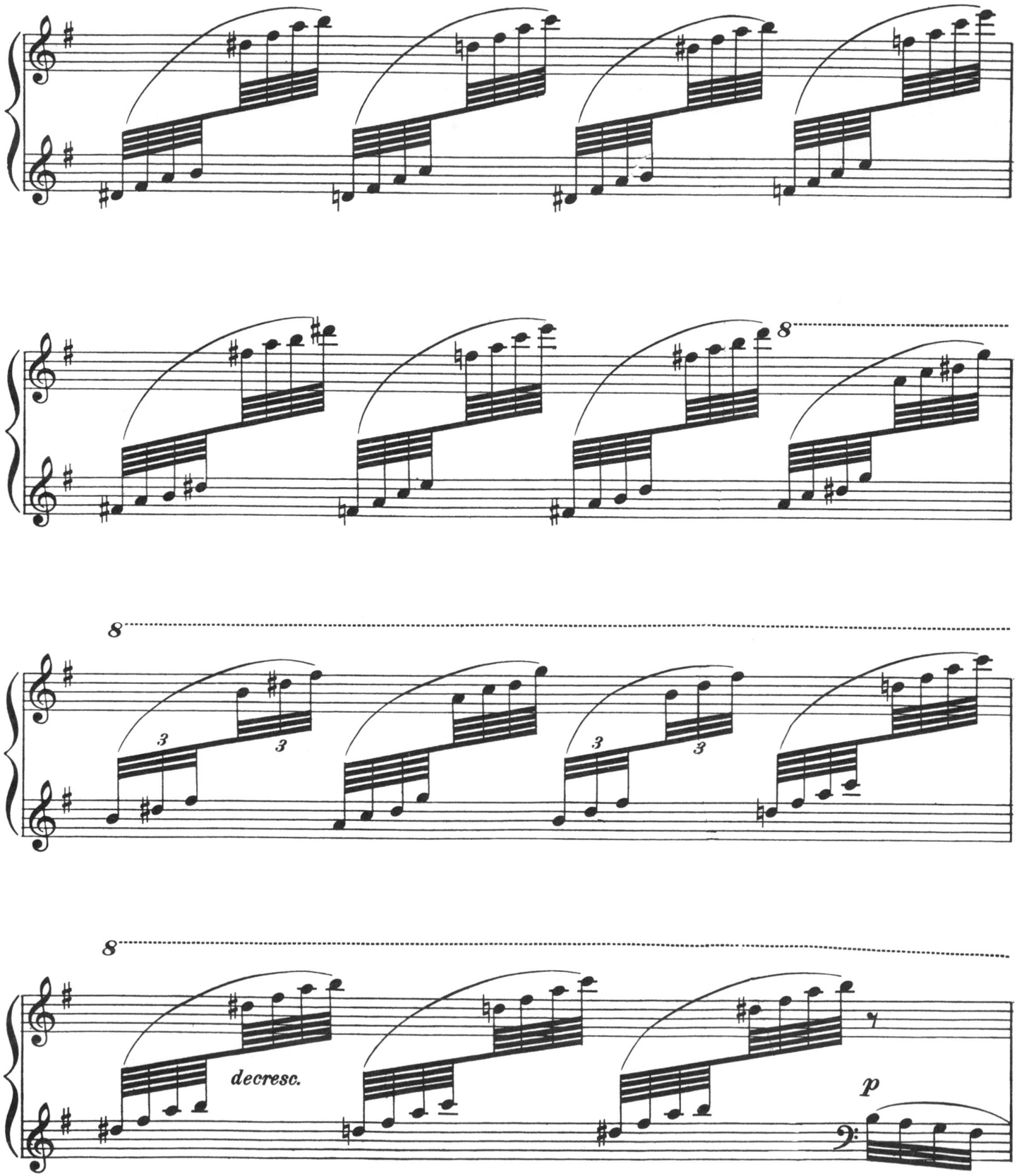
8
8
3
3
3
3
8
decresc.
p

pp delicatissimo
Ped.
mp
pp
sempre
pp
f

Russian Dance, "Trepak"

ff mf
cresc.
ff
p pesante
cresc.
ff
f
ff
ff
mf
ff
mf
ff
mf
ff
ff
fff

sfz mf
ffz mf
f
stringendo cresc. poco a poco
ff
cresc.
Prestissimo
ff
cresc.
fff
sfz

Arabian Dance

pp
5
pp
5
p
mf
5
5
p
mf
5
5
p
pp
5
p
pp
5

mf
f
p
mf
5
dolce
p
f
mf
p
mf
5
p
p
5
mf
p
5
mp
pp
5
p
pp poco a poco
morendo sin' al Fine
ppp

Chinese Dance

f
mf
tr
f
tr
mf
f
cresc.
ff

Dance of the Reed Flutes

p
p
mp
delicato
p
mf
sempre stacc.
p
mp
mf
p
mf
cresc.
f
p
Ped.
Ped.
*

leggero e staccato
p

p
sempre stacc.
mf
p
mp
mf
p
mf
p
cresc.
ff

Waltz of the Flowers

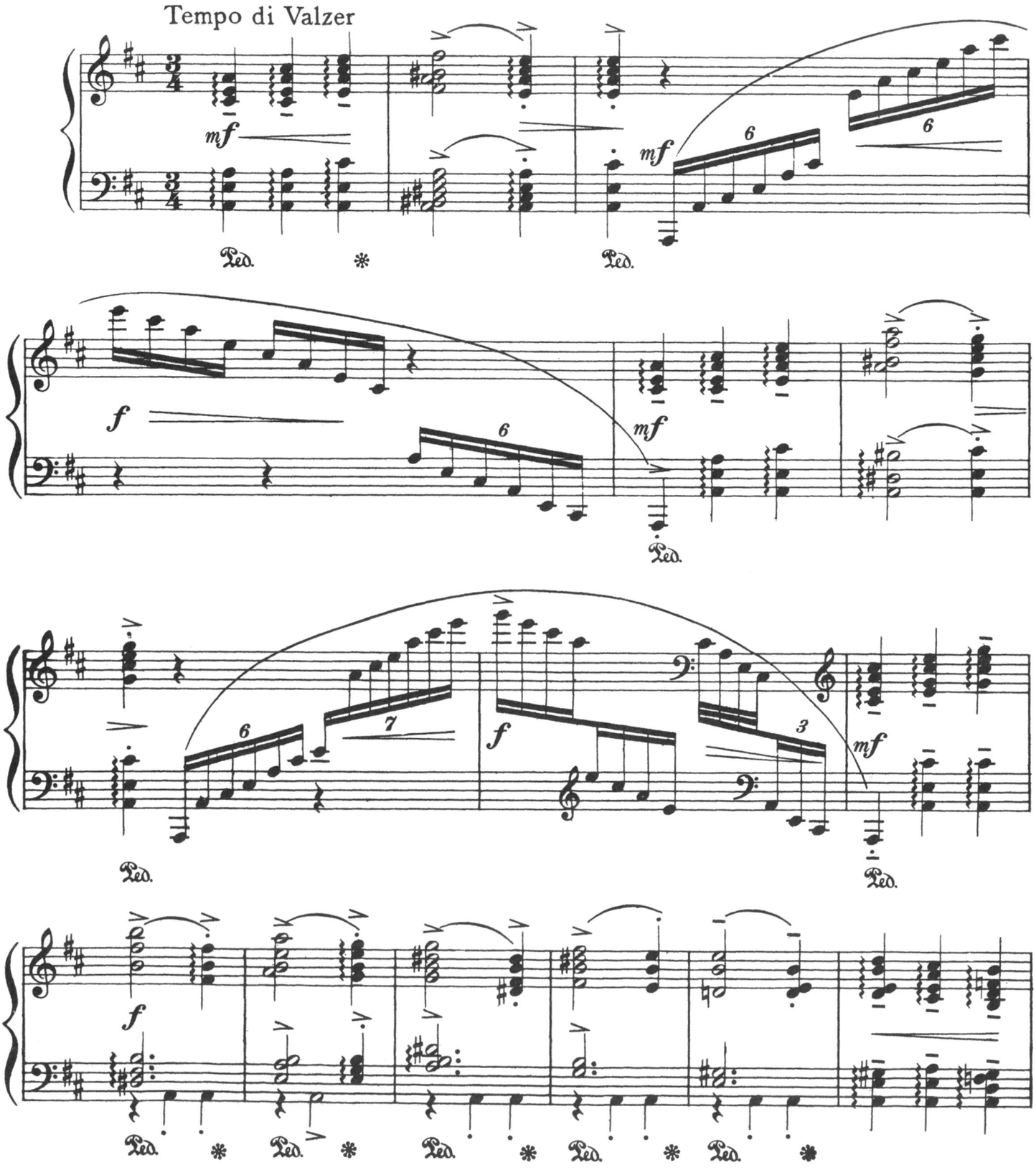

Cadenza
f
a piacere
p trem.
con Pedale
mf
mf
f
cresc.
ff
sfz
rit.
smorzando

a tempo
pp leggero
dolce cantando
p
ten.
f
p
cresc.
mf
p
mp
ten.
p
mf

f
dolce
Ped. *
sfz
f cantando
Ped. *
f
1.
sfz
2.
sfz
dolce

cantabile
mf
p
mf
ten.
f
p dolce cantando
p
ten.
f

Con anima
f
mf non legato
f
mf
Ped.
ff
8
p dolce
Ped.

8
p
8
mp
ten.
cresc.
f
più f
ff
3
pp
p
ten.
f

p
cresc.
mf
p
ten.
p
mf
f

dolce
f
sfz
f cantando
Ped.
f
f
ff

sfz
p subito
stacc.
mp
pp
cresc.
cresc.
espress.
sfz
ff
Ped.
*
Ped.
*
sfz

ff
8
3
ff
p subito
cresc.
f
ff

8
ff
p subito
cresc.
f
sfz
ff
brillante
sfz
sfz
sfz accel. e cresc.
sfz
fff
8
sfz
sfz
Ped.
*

LABORUM
DULCE
LENIMEN
G. SCHIRMER

The Seasons
Opus 37b

JANUARY

By the Hearth

Edited and fingered by
Louis Oesterle

Pyotr Il'yich Tchaikovsky
Op. 37a

Copyright © 1909, Renewed 1937 by G. Schirmer, Inc. (ASCAP) New York, NY
International Copyright Secured. All Rights Reserved.
Warning: Unauthorized reproduction of this publication is prohibited by Federal law and subject to criminal prosecution.

poco cresc.
mf
dim.
p
Ped.
p
riten.
poco più f

Meno mosso
p molto espress.
leggierissimo
pp
p
pp
p
pp
p
mf
espr.
poco riten.
mf

p a tempo
pp
p
pp
p
poco string
dim.
riten.

Tempo I
p
Ped.
poco più f
p
poco cresc.
mf
dim.
p

p
Ped.
cresc.
mf
p
poco riten.
ppp
Ped.
Ped.
8
ppp
Ped.
ppp

FEBRUARY

Carnival

f
Ped.
p
cresc.
cresc.
f
Ped.
Ped.
Ped.
Ped.

f
ff
p
poco a poco cresc.
ff

L'istesso tempo
f
p
Ped.

p
cresc.
f
ff
p

cresc. poco a poco
ff
mf
p
p
pp
fff

MARCH

Song of the Lark

p
dim.
poco ritenuto
a tempo
p
pp
pp
ppp

APRIL

Snowdrop

Edited and fingered by
Louis Oesterle

più
f
p
con grazia
p
p
p
p
mf
p
rit.
Ped.

a tempo
p
Ped.
mf
dim.
a tempo
p dolce
rit.
poco cresc.

mf
rit.
p
marcato la melodia
a tempo
poco cresc.
più
f
dim.
pp
morendo si poco a poco
ppp

MAY

Starlit Night

Allegro giocoso
mf
p
Ped.

cresc.
poco
ritard.
poco meno mosso
f
dim.
Tempo I
mf
dim.

ritard.
Andantino
p
poco cresc.
pp
poco rit.
p a tempo
p espress.
pp
ppp

JUNE

Barcarolle

Edited and fingered by
Louis Oesterle

cresc.
f
dim.
p
espress.
cresc.
dim.
Poco più mosso.
p ma poco a poco cresc.
f

Allegro giocoso.
più f
f
sf
p
cresc.
stringendo.
ff poco riten.
8
Tempo I.
f
rall.
Andante cantabile.
a tempo.
espress.

dim.
p
espress.
poco più f
dim.
p
cresc.
f
dim.
p
p
espress.
cresc.

dim.
p
poco cresc.
espress.
dim.
p
p
pp
un poco cresc.
pp

JULY

Song of the Reaper

ff
poco dim.
mf

Ped.
poco a poco dim.
pp

AUGUST

Harvest Song

cresc.
f
p
poco
cresc.
f

Ped.
ff
mf
cresc.
ff
p
marcato poco cresc.

mf
pespress.
cresc.
mf
dim.
p
poco cresc.
mf
p
pp

p
Ped.
mf
p

cresc.
f
Ped.
Ped.
p
poco cresc.
f
Ped.

Ped.
ff
nf
cresc.
8
ff

SEPTEMBER

Hunter's Song

Ped.
p
poco cresc.
mf

f
p
f
nf
f
ff
f
f

cresc.
ff
Ped.

OCTOBER

Autumn Song

p
poco cresc.
mf
rit.
a tempo
p

poco cresc.
dim.
p marcato
poco più f
dim.
pp
morendo
pppp

NOVEMBER

Troika

cresc.
f
dim.
p
grazioso
mf
sf
p
sf
p
sf

mf
sf
p
sf
p
sf
p
sf
mf
sf
p
sf
p
sf
mf
sf
p
sf
p
sf
p cresc.
f dimin. poco a poco

sempre stacc.
p poco marcata la mano sinistra.
p espress
r.h.

staccato
p
p
dimin.
pp

DECEMBER

Christmas

p
Ped.
mf
dim.
molto rit.
a tempo
poco cresc.
simile

molto rit.
a tempo
p
cresc.
mf
p
p
Ped.
f
mf
f
mf

p
poco cresc.
mf
p
poco cresc.
simile

molto rit.
a tempo
p
poco cresc.
molto rit.
a tempo
p
p
Ped.
Ped.
Ped.

p
mf
Ped.
p
mf
Ped.
dim.
p
Ped.
molto rit.
a tempo
poco cresc.
p
Ped.
Ped. simile
molto rit.

a tempo
p
cresc.
mf
p
poco a poco cresc.
f
mf
p

Other Selected Piano Pieces
From Opuses 2, 5, 10, 19, and 40

RÊVERIE DU SOIR

Edited and fingered by
Louis Oesterle

Pyotr Il'yich Tchaikovsky
Op. 19, No. 1

espress.
pp
L'istesso tempo.
p
mf
mf
p
mf

p
Ped.
più f
mf
p
mf

p
pp
espr.
Ped.
tr
p
ppp
Fine.

LABORUM
DULCE
LENIMEN
G. SCHIRMER

CHANT SANS PAROLES

Pyotr Il'yich Tchaikovsky
Op. 2, No 3

p
cresc.
f
f
dim.
poco rit.
p
marc.
Tempo I.

f
energico
cresc.
ff
dim.
p
f

cresc.
ff
dim.
p
p
sempre di - mi - nu - en - do
marcata la melodia
pp
ppp

ROMANCE

Pyotr Il'yich Tchaikovsky
Op. 5

poco più mosso.
crescendo.
riten.
a
mf
mf
tempo.
cresc.
f
p
pp
poco a poco accel. -
cresc. - - - -

Allegro energico.
mf
f
ff

8
m. s.
m. d.
molto meno mosso.
m.s.
m.d.
mf
dimin.
p
Tempo I.
espr.
pp

p
marcato.
Ped.
mf
espr.
poco più mosso.
cresc.
mf
riten.
a
mf

tempo.
molto più
f
mosso dimin.
Allegro.
p
ritard.

NOCTURNE

Pyotr Il'yich Tchaikovsky
Op. 10, No. 1

pp
cresc.
mf
ten.
cresc.
mf
ten.
p
mf
f
p

p
mf
cresc.
dim.
pp

pp leggiero.
mf
pp
p
poco cresc.
dim.
p
pp

HUMORESQUE

Pyotr Il'yich Tchaikovsky
Op. 10, No. 2

Semplice, ma espress.
cresc.
mf
dim.
p
pp
poco cresc. rit.
sf
p

pp
rit.
poco cresc.
mf
a
tempo
rit.
poco più
f
mf
a tempo
p
stacc.

cresc.
ff
stacc.
p
cresc.
sempre stacc.
poco
a poco dim.

FEUILLET D'ALBUM

Pyotr Il'yich Tchaikovsky
Op. 19, No. 3

p
cresc.
f
p
p
mf
p
pp

CHANSON TRISTE

Edited and fingered by
W. K. Bassford

Pyotr Il'yich Tchaikovsky
Op. 40, No. 2

f
p
poco rit.
p a tempo
f
p
mf
p
pp
ppp

CHANT SANS PAROLES

Pyotr Il'yich Tchaikovsky
Op. 40, No. 6

f
p
p

mf
cresc.
marcato.
f
dim.
p
p
pp
poco rall.
pp